BICYCLE MAINTENANCE & REPAIR

Frames/Tires/Wheels

Text by Richard E. Mahoney
Introduction and Photography by Forest H. Belt

THEODORE AUDEL & CO.
a division of
HOWARD W. SAMS & CO., INC.
4300 West 62nd Street
Indianapolis, Indiana 46268

FIRST EDITION

FIRST PRINTING—1974

Copyright © 1974 by Howard W. Sams & Co., Inc., Indianapolis, Indiana 46268. Printed in the United States of America.

International Standard Book Number: 0-672-23806-3

Contents

SECTION 1

Introduction

Ten-speed bicycles have proliferated. Around 60 million travel the highways and byways, and riders buy nearly 15 million new ones each year. That adds up to a lot of bicycle wear and tear. And repair bills . . .

To save money, owners who ride a lot naturally attempt many of their own repairs. Once they become experienced, they save quite a lot. But trial and error make expensive teachers. Many things about a bicycle are not at all hard to repair — that is, if you know how. The detailed guidance in this book, profusely supported by closeup photographs, can help you avoid costly difficulties.

Richard E. Mahoney, the bicycle technician who helped with the photography and supplied the technical expertise for this guidebook, knows ten-speed bicycles inside-out. For every dollar you save repairing and adjusting your ten-speed, you owe him a vote of thanks.

A word about how the book is arranged. Buyers find some ten-speed bicycles delivered in a box. Some bike dealers will assemble them for you. But when you buy at some stores, you have to put the complex-appearing machine together yourself.

Don't despair. With care and some direction, you can assemble the handlebars, brake levers, pedals, and the like. Plus, you will find a lot of general adjustments to be made.

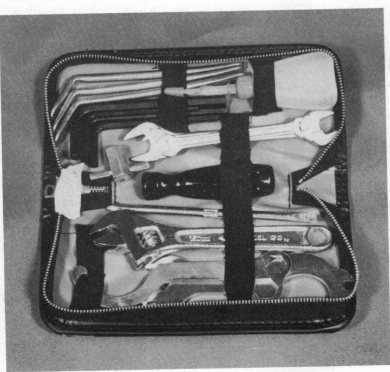

You need a few tools. You can buy them as a kit from your bicycle dealers. Not just any tools will do. Multispeed bikes use hardware in metric sizes. All of the work and adjustments apply equally to any machine you have been riding. In sections, the explanations elaborate on maintenance as well as adjustment.

There are two books in this series. Book one covers handlebars, saddles, tires and wheel assembly and adjustments—book two covers brakes, chain repair and maintenance and the derailleur mechanism.

In either book, you will find all the aid you need to maintain, adjust, and repair your own ten-speed bicycle. With these photos to show you where and how, you should have the best operating bike around.

Adjusting Fork, Wheels, and Cranks

Check the bag of parts you receive with a new bike. A packing list in the carton should tell you what is supplied. No use beginning the project with some key part missing. You should at least find saddle, stem, handlebars, brake levers, pedals, and reflectors. The bike may include safety levers, kickstand, and other accessories.

A workshop helps immensely. So much of the work, both assembly and adjustment, can be performed easier at waist level than on the floor or ground. (Avoid grassy plots; small hardware disappears too easily.) Lacking a stand, you can suspend the frame from rafters or hooks with a rope. Loop the rope around the head tube (above the front wheel). Run it over the rafter or hooks to the seat tube (where top tube, seat tube, and rear wheel stays join). You will find advantages far beyond the saving of wear and tear on your back and legs.

Before you begin attaching parts, go through some preliminary checks. Certain assemblies need adjustment. For example, the fork. This member holds the front wheel. Cones, bearings, and cups at the top and bottom of the bicycle head tube hold the upper extremity of the fork. You can adjust the head cones, if they need it. Here's how to decide.

Grasp the wheel from directly in front. Hold the head tube steady and pull on the front wheel. Listen for clicks, however slight, inside the head tube. Any clicking means the cones

that support the fork have been left too loose. There should be no room for the fork to rattle even a tiny bit.

If you hear no clicks that signify looseness, try pushing the front wheel from side to side, pivoting the fork. The weight of the tire and wheel should swivel the fork with no help from you. If the fork and wheel stop on their own anywhere but

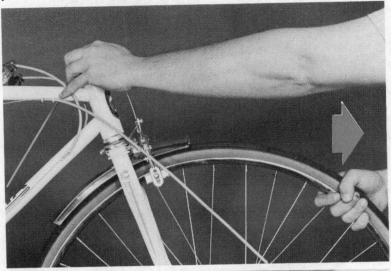

dead center (balanced), the cones are too tight. You'll have trouble steering the bicycle. You should test the fork before every major ride. You'll forestall excessive wear on head cones and bearings.

Adjusting the head cone is simple. First you loosen the head/fork locknut. It's the large nut at the very top of the head tube. Be easy with it; you can mar its chrome finish if you use *Channellock®* pliers instead of a wrench. This may be one of the few nuts on the bicycle that takes a standard-size wrench instead of a metric size. It's also easily managed with an adjustable wrench. Loosen it counterclockwise.

A knurled wheel just below the locknut constitutes the cone adjustment. Tighten or loosen the cones. Best procedure: loosen the adjustment enough that you can hear clicks when you pull forward on the front wheel. Then tighten down the cone just enough to eliminate that ever-so-slight rattle.

Recheck to make sure the fork turns freely, falling sideways at the slightest tap. (This test demonstrates the advisability of having a stand or suspending the bike. You cannot test the fork correctly with the bike frame standing on the ground.) Retighten the locknut, and again check to be sure the knurled wheel hasn't moved when the locknut was tightened.

Next, check the crank and its hanger. In construction and adjustment, they resemble the fork and head tube. That is— cones, bearings, and cups in the hanger hold the crank solidly, yet free to rotate smoothly and without binding.

Testing procedure runs much the same as for the fork, too. You grasp the pedal arms and try shaking the crank laterally in the hanger. Even the slightest click tells you the cones are loose. Left that way, the crank wears out the hanger bearings sooner than it should. At its worst, this looseness makes pedaling dangerous and a waste of your energy.

Assuming you hear or feel no clicks, rotate the crank and chainwheels. Flip one pedal arm with a finger. The assembly should spin freely at the slightest shove. Move the crank this way several revolutions. You should feel no binding at any spot. If you do, inspect the washer under the crank locknut. It might not be exactly round, or it might have a malformed key; either can let it rub the crank hanger tube slightly.

To make a cone adjustment, you must remove the crank locknut and washer (which doubles as a dustcover). Notice the direction the locknut unscrews (or is removed): it's clockwise, because the crank has a left-hand thread. This is true

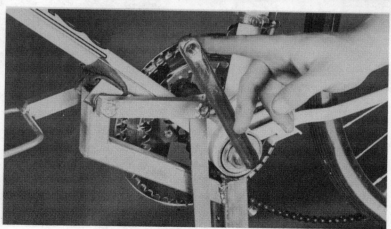

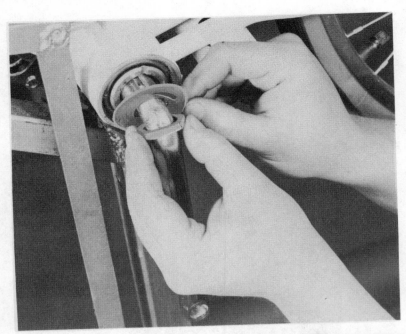

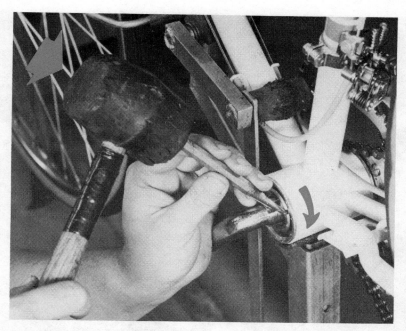

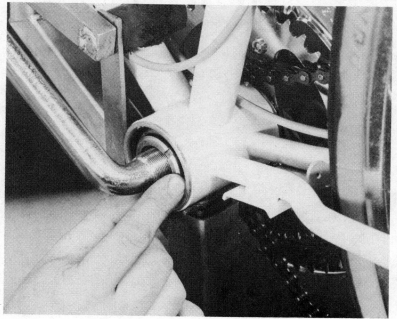

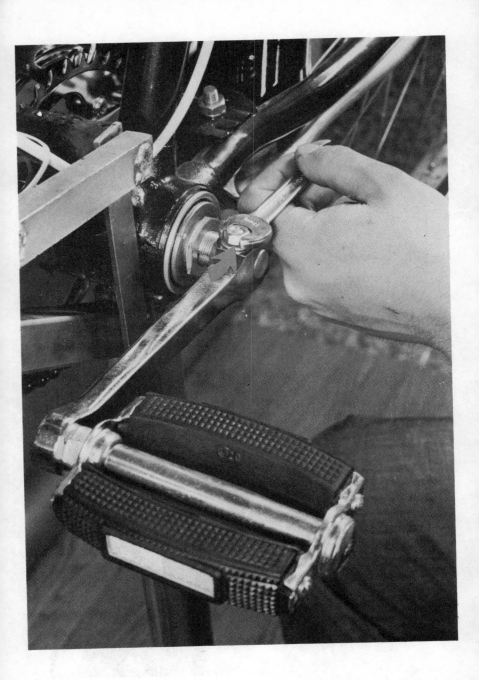

of all one-piece cranks such as this. If you found the dust-cover washer eccentric or slightly off-center during your testing, toss it away and substitute a new one.

Threads on the cone are also left-hand. Notches on the cone give you a means for adjustment. If the cone is too tight and binds the crank, you'll have to back it off slightly. That means you turn the cone clockwise. Use a flat-tipped punch and light taps with a mallet to rotate the cone.

When the cone appears too loose, letting the crank click slightly in the hanger, you can usually turn the cone with your fingers. Twist it counterclockwise to tighten it. Replace the dustcover washer and the locknut. Tighten the locknut counterclockwise, and recheck the crank for smooth turning.

Three-piece steel cranks come on many imported bikes. The *cottered* type is most common, having a tapered cotter pin bolted through the pedal arm. The cotter pin wedges into a slanted groove near the end of the crank spindle. You may have trouble knocking the pin out.

If you must remove the pedal arm for any reason, start by backing the nut off until it is flush with the end of the cotter pin threads. That way, hitting it with a hammer will not mar or flatten the threads. Don't sledge-hammer the pin. A few sharp light taps of the hammer will jar the pin loose.

Place a flat-ended drive punch against the threaded end of the cotter pin. A few more taps with the hammer should loosen the pin enough that you can pull it out with your fingers.

The tapered wedge on the crank spindle and the wedge shape of the pin bind them together tightly. They do not come apart easily—yet you must be very careful. If you damage the cotter pin getting it out, put in a new one. Reinstalling a warped or marred cotter pin makes removing it the next time almost impossible. You might even ruin the crank spindle and bearings in the effort.

Adjusting the cone in the crank hanger requires that you loosen a locknut, just as with one-piece cranks. Remember, the thread is left-hand, when loosening, go clockwise. One difference is that the cone forms its own dustcover in this three-piece design.

Behind the locknut, the cone contains indentations you can use with the flat punch. Loosen the cones by turning the exposed cone clockwise. Do not loosen it so much that the crank gets wobbly. Remember, you want no clicks, but no binding either. Tighten the cone, when that's needed, by tapping it counterclockwise very lightly. It's easy to overtighten, and you should retest the crank laterally and rotationally at every step.

When the adjusting is finished, reinstall the crank locknut. Be cautious when tightening the nut; do not throw the cone out of adjustment. In turning the locknut to tighten, you could move the cone a hair.

One other point. You do not always have to remove the pedal arm to reach the crank hanger cone adjustment—but you need a thin wrench to get at the locknut if you choose to make the adjustment with the pedals on. There is one case where the pedals must be removed—this is when repacking the bearings inside the hanger with fine axle grease. Ordinarily this once-a-year job belongs to an experienced technician. Yet, if you completely back out the cones on both sides of the crank hanger (clockwise on the left side; counterclockwise on the right), you have access to the bearings. Squeeze them full of grease and then wipe off the excess.

Restore the pedal arm and the cotter pin carefully. Forcible pounding here can ruin pedal alignment. Work the cotter pin into the groove with your fingers first, while wiggling the pedal arm. Then tap lightly with the hammer or mallet, still shaking the pedal arm so the cotter pin fits smoothly and tightly into the wedge groove. Install the lockwasher and nut on the cotter pin and tighten the nut firmly.

Lightweight foreign bikes may use a cotterless aluminum three-piece crank. The crank spindle contains large splines near the end. These spindles, and a bolt through the pedal arm, key the arm to the crank spindle solidly so they turn together. A nut at the end of the crank spindle holds the pedal arm on tightly. If the pedal arm can wobble or click even slightly on the spindle, tighten that nut. A dust cap covers this nut.

You can adjust hanger cones without removing the pedals. The locking binder for the cones is a ring concentric to the

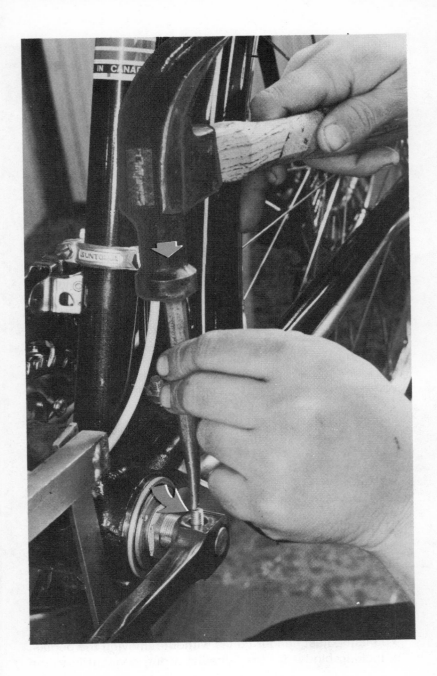

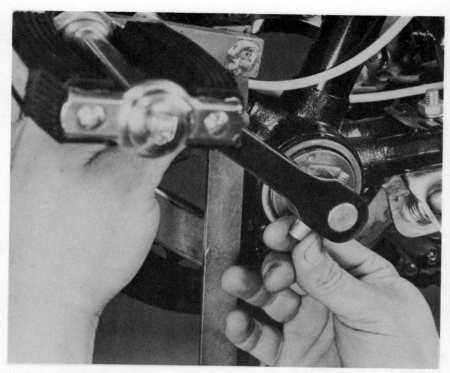

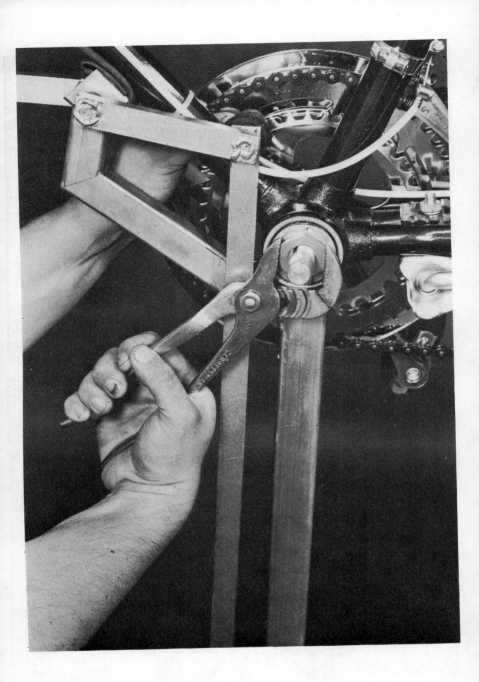

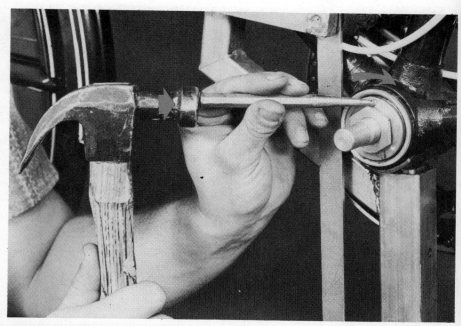

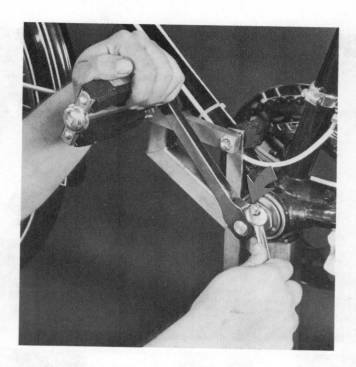

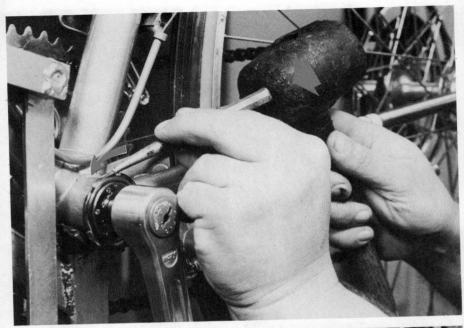

cone adjustment itself. You tap it lightly with your flat punch and a mallet. **NOTE:** In this one instance, the thread runs standard. Therefore, to loosen the locking ring, tap it counterclockwise.

The cone also has standard threads. If the crank clicks when you shake it laterally, showing looseness, tighten the cone slightly by rotating it clockwise. If the crank turns sluggishly, rotate the cone counterclockwise just enough to free the spindle. Do not forget to retighten the locking ring when you are finished.

When assembling a bicycle, put the pedals on after you know the crank is in proper adjustment. Pedals are stamped with **L** and **R** for left and right. Be sure each goes on the side where it belongs. Outside of that, the procedure is simple.

Oil the threads—this will not keep the threads from rusting, but it does keep them from seizing in the pedal arm. Later, if you ever need to replace a damaged pedal you will not need a whole new crank.

Screw the pedals into the crank arm. Left-pedal threads are left-hand, so the nub screws in counterclockwise. Right-pedal threads are standard. Tightening either one takes a thin-profile wrench. Tighten them firmly, but do not overdo it. If the pedal bearings and cones are okay, the threads will not unscrew from the pedal arm easily.

European pedals essentially install the same way. They are generally built with greater precision and can be dismantled for adjustment. This task seems easier with the pedal on the crank arm.

Start by taking off the dustcover. Some are hexagon, some are round. The latter may get scarred if you are not careful. The threads are standard so remove the cover counterclockwise. Inside the dustcover, you will find the usual arrangement. A locknut covers the cone. Your first step: unscrew that locknut. A metric box-end wrench reaches the nut okay, despite the fact it is recessed.

Behind the locknut you will find a keyed washer. Fish it loose with your pocketknife or some other thin, flat tool. Sharpnose pliers can be used to grip and remove the washer. This exposes the cone.

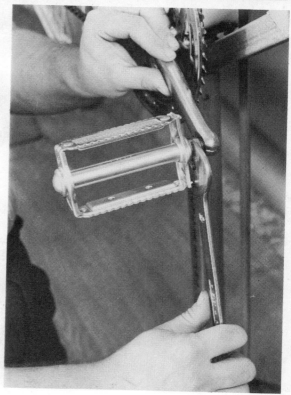

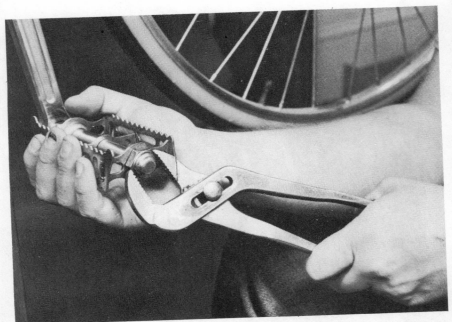

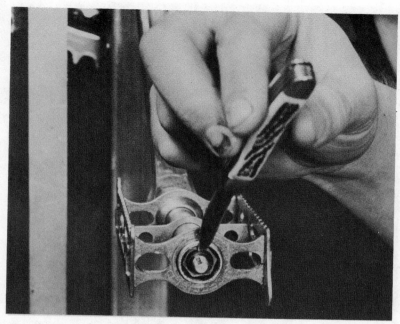

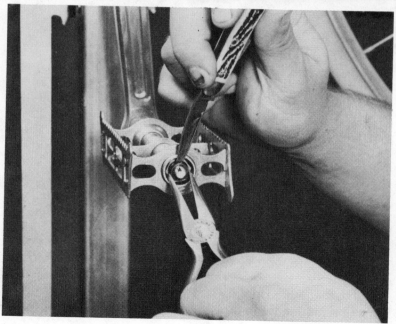

Although the cone shoulder has a hex shape, a box-end wrench can't fit deep enough to reach the hex. There is not enough clearance around the edges for the walls of the wrench. So you make the adjustment with the same flat thin tool you used to remove the washer.

Try pushing/pulling the pedal gently. If you hear clicks, the cone needs tightening (clockwise). Spin the pedal. If it's sluggish, loosen the cone slightly. When you are satisfied the pedal turns smoothly and freely, without end play, replace the washer and dustcover.

You can install toe clips on most metal (called rat-trap) pedals. It only takes a few minutes. Toe clips consist of a metal toe guard, usually of polished spring steel, and a shoe strap.

A thin metal backing plate bolts to the mounting plate. Remove the mounting plate and the bolts and slip the backing

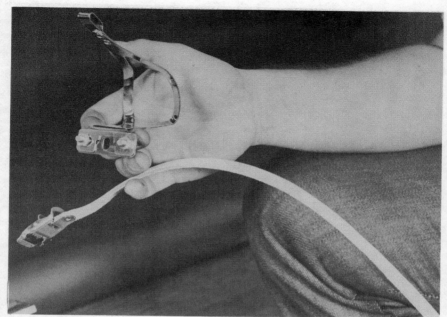

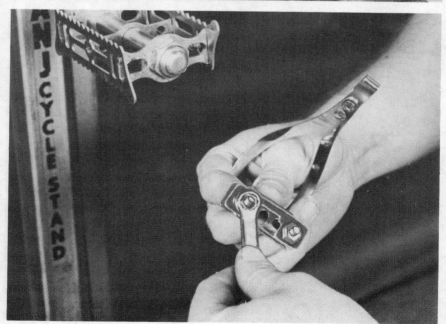

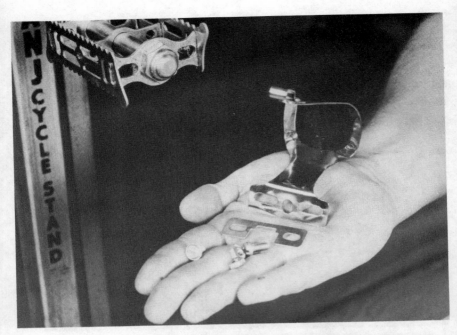

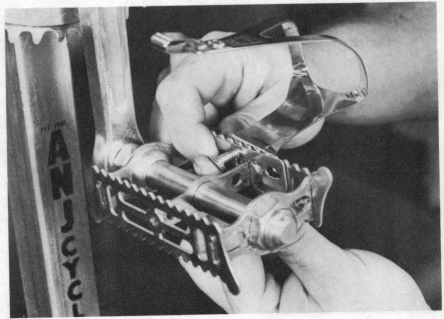

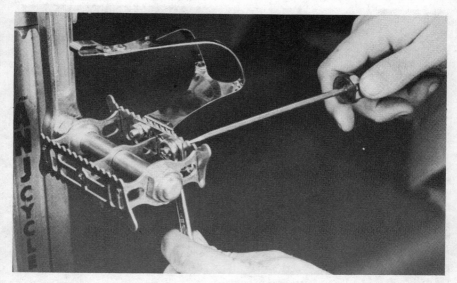

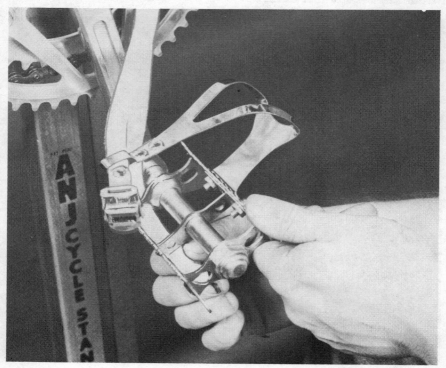

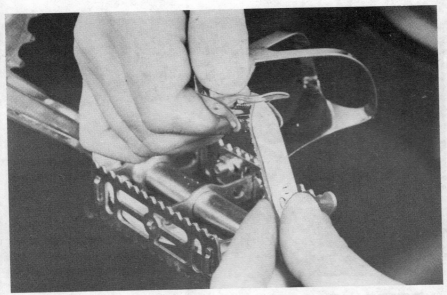

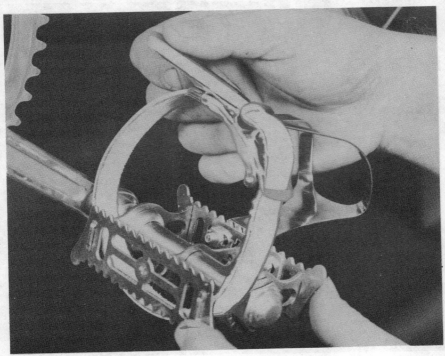

plate inside the pedal. Insert the bolts through the mounting plate of the toe guard, the pedal riser, and the backing plate. Slip lockwashers on the two bolts, then install and tighten the nuts.

Make them very tight. Toe clips absorb a lot of punishment. They are critical to safety, and you do not want them coming loose.

Next, you thread the strap. It goes through the rear loop of the toe guard, toward the chainwheel (outside the edge of the pedal) and into the rear slot in the pedal's inside riser. From there it goes across and out the same slot in the outside riser. Thence up to the buckle.

Pinch the buckle open and insert the strap end. Adjust the strap to fit your shoes. If you change shoes, change the strap setting. Your foot should come out easily, yet not rattle around inside the cage formed by the toe guard and strap. However, for safety in a fall, better too loose than too tight.

Next in order, examine the front wheel hub. Grasp one side of the fork in one hand to steady it. Grip the top of the wheel with your other hand. Gently try to shake the wheel. This intermittent pressure reveals any lateral looseness in the hub. You can hear or feel the hub click back and forth if the cones need tightening.

Cones in the hub might be too tight. You can check this only with the bicycle suspended, in a stand or from ropes. Rotate the wheel until you are holding the valve stem exactly horizontal. Release your grip on the wheel. The weight of the valve stem pulls downward and rotates the wheel if the hub does not bind. If the wheel does not rotate freely, you must loosen the cones.

Front wheel spindles hang in the same cup/bearing/cone arrangement you find in the fork, crank, pedals, and any other rotating part of the bicycle. You correct looseness or tightness by changing the cone tension. Remove the wheel by loosening the outside (axle) nut on each side of the fork.

Next to the hub itself you will find another nut. This is the locknut for the cones. There is a cone on either side of the hub, but you only need to adjust one. (If the wheel hub is far off-center, curing it is generally a job for your bicycle expert.) Loosen the locknut on one side.

Here is a quick way to get the adjustment right: Loosen the cone until you can hear a click as you pull back and forth on the spindle. Then retighten the cone until the click just disappears. Grab the spindle with your fingers and give it a twist. It should spin a few turns with no binding whatever. Put the locknut back down tight. Recheck the adjustment by spinning the axle or spindle. If it is still free, you are ready to put the wheel back into the fork.

Install the threaded spindle ends in the fork dropout slots with the locknut inside and the axle nut outside. Lockwashers go between the outside nut and the fork arm. Tighten the nuts barely enough to hold the wheel. Align the wheel so the top is exactly in the center of the fork. Then tighten the outside nuts. Recheck centering at the top.

You check the rear wheel hub just as you did the front. Turn the wheel until the valve stem stands horizontal, between the chain stays. Release your grip and the stem weight should rotate the wheel till the stem is at the bottom. If the wheel sticks, you know the hub cones are too tight. Grab the wheel and try moving it backward and forward. Clicks in the hub tell you the cones are too loose.

You will have to remove the wheel. Rear wheel removal involves a lot more work than taking off the front wheel. Start by loosening the axle nuts outside the dropout slots on each side of the hub. Hold onto the wheel if you loosen these nuts very far; you are not ready for it to fall out yet. Grasp the derailleur arm and twist it backward, against its spring tension. That may release the wheel. With some, you still have to push forward and downward to slide the wheel out of the dropout slots. Lift the chain out of the derailleur and off the cogwheel cluster and the wheel is clear for adjustment.

You will find the adjustment for cones in the rear hub on the side opposite the cog cluster. As usual, there is a locknut, and this one is fairly tight. Grip the end of the spindle just beyond the cog cluster with the round shank in a pair of pliers, to keep the spindle from turning as you loosen the locknut.

Loosen the cone adjusting nut, all the while keeping your grip on the opposite end of the spindle. When there is enough slack in the cones to let you shake the spindle back and

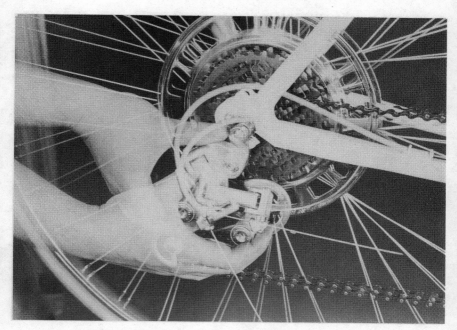

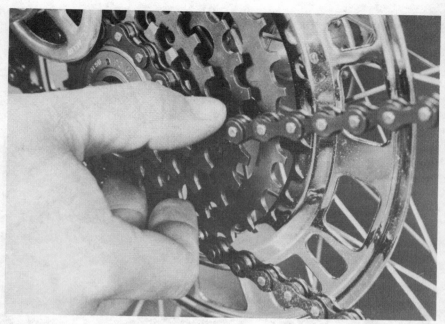

45

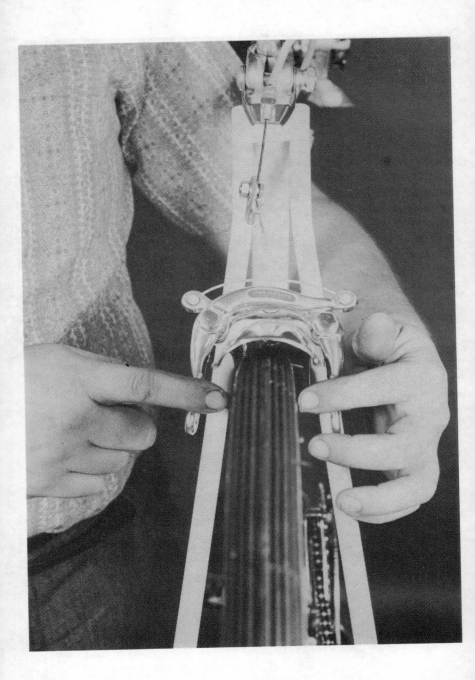

forth (listen for or feel the clicks), begin tightening the cone adjustment. Snug it up just enough to eliminate the sideways play, but not enough to cause binding. Twist the spindle to

make sure it's free. It should "coast" a few revolutions when you give it a vigorous twist.

Retighten the locknut. You are ready to remount the wheel and align it in the stays.

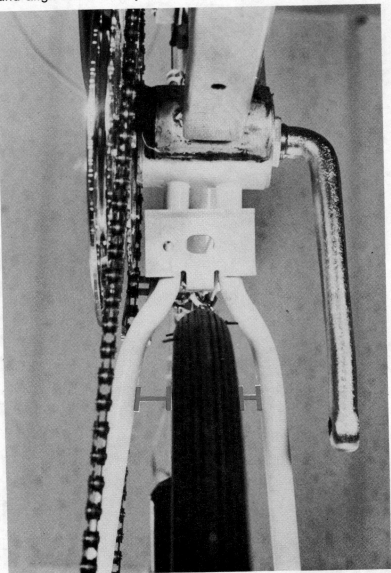

Screw the axle nuts on the spindle ends before you lift the wheel. Be sure the lockwasher is inside each nut. Hang the chain over the smallest cog.

Raise the wheel straight up, and it might roll the derailleur back out of the way itself. Or, you may have to pull the derailleur backward. Be sure it has all the spring tension it had to start with. You might have to rotate some derailleurs a full turn and then pull them back. Thread the chain back into the derailleur roller bar.

Watch the positions of the nut and lockwasher as the spindle slides into the dropout slots. The washer must be on the outside, next to the nut. Inside the stays, this washer can mess up operation. Pull the wheel spindle into the dropout slots. Snug the axle nuts against the slots, but do not tighten them yet.

Verify that the chain follows its proper path through the derailleur and over the cogs. There should be no binding of either chain or wheel.

Now align the rear wheel. The wheel and tire should center precisely between the chain stays and between the seat stays. You can align the wheel by sliding the spindle bolts in the dropout slots. When you have the wheel exactly aligned at both points, tighten the axle nuts.

IMPORTANT NOTE: While front and rear wheels are off, you might take them to a bicycle shop that can check for perfect roundness and for wobble. Either deficiency strains the bicycle frame and wears tires badly. Some cases can even make the bike dangerous to ride.

While you are at the wheels, check tire pressure. No one pressure suits all tires. Fortunately, most bicycle tires have the proper pressure stamped on the sidewall. If your tires do not show proper pressure, put 60 lb. in them—that's enough for safety.

Check fender mountings. Fender bolts have a habit of coming loose. You will find them at any of several places. They may fasten the front fender stays at the fender, the front fender at the fork, the rear fender at the seat stays, the rear fender at the chain stays, and both rear fender stays at the fender. Reflectors on fenders and on wheels should be attached solidly and checked regularly.

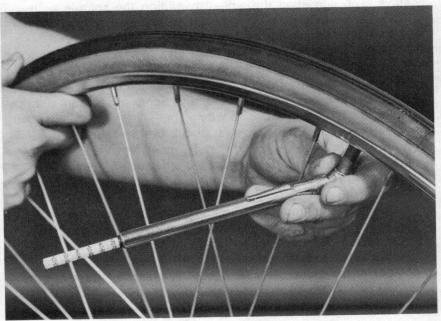

SECTION 3

Handlebars and Saddles

Up front, the first thing you install is the stem. This is what holds the handlebars. The stem comes already assembled, two pieces of metal with a bolt through the center. The ends next to each other are wedge-shaped. When you tighten the bolt with the stem inside the fork barrel (which is inside the head tube), the wedge forces the diameter wider and binds the stem and fork tightly together. They turn as one piece in the head tube.

A majority of bicycles have gear shifters mounted on the stem. During assembly, you must slip the collar of the shifters onto the stem. Slide them up near the angled neck of the stem, and lightly tighten the collar so it cannot slip around.

Prepare the stem for inserting into the top (head) of the fork. Make sure the bolt is loose and the two sections align straight. Smear the stem with oil. This, as with the pedal threads mentioned earlier, prevents the stem from seizing inside the fork. With or without the oil, the stem is prone to rust, but the oil keeps the rusted surfaces apart enough that you can pull the stem out for servicing or repair. You may not have to repair a fork or stem often, but pulling the stem out for inspection and reoiling should be part of yearly maintenance.

When you insert the stem in the head tube, notice the depth indicator line embossed in the metal. This is a gauge by which you know how deep to push the stem. Some stems do not have this indicator on the stem so rule of thumb is: Leave as much of the stem down inside the fork as shows above the head nut. That way, when you put pressure on the handle-

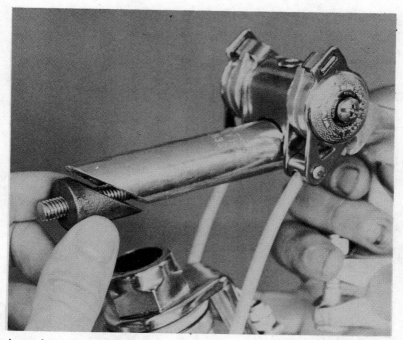

bars for some reason, the stem is not likely to snap off. Using the indicator line as a gauge, push the stem deep enough that the line is out of sight.

Tighten the stem nut. That expands the wedge near the bottom of the stem and grips the fork barrel inside the head tube. Do not tighten too much—leave the stem so you can move it. Line it up so the neck points forward, and slide the shifter levers around so they are centered. Do not tighten the stem or shifter levers at this time—this can be done after handlebars are installed and aligned.

Ten-speed bikes with the racing frame use *maes-bend* handlebars. They are also known as *drop* handlebars. Starting at either end, thread the handlebar into the clamp in the neck of the stem. At the center of the straight portion of the handlebar, you will see fine splines. Slip those into the clamp, exactly centered, then lightly tighten the clamp bolt.

Twist the stem so the long straightaway part of the handlebars aligns exactly perpendicular to the front wheels. Snug the stem bolt down a little tighter.

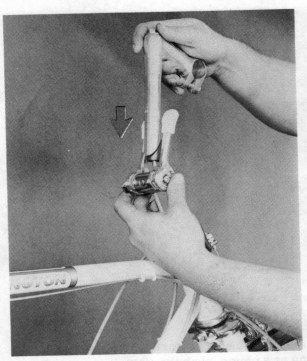

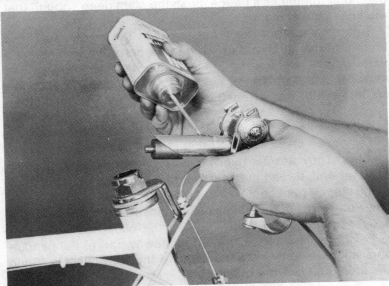

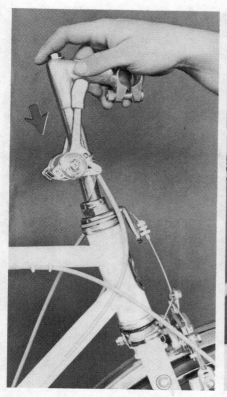

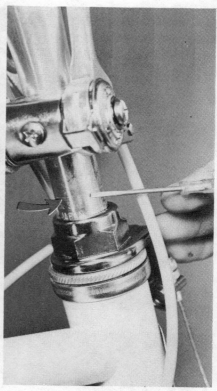

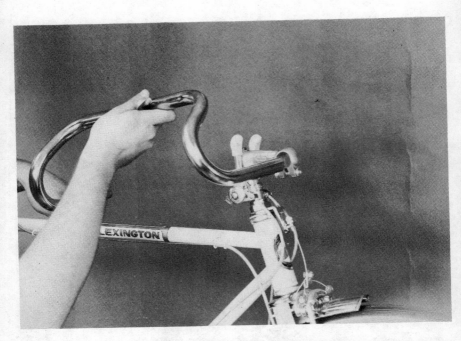

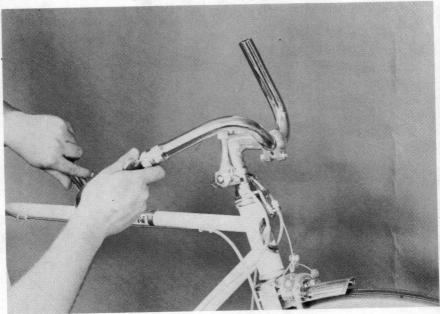

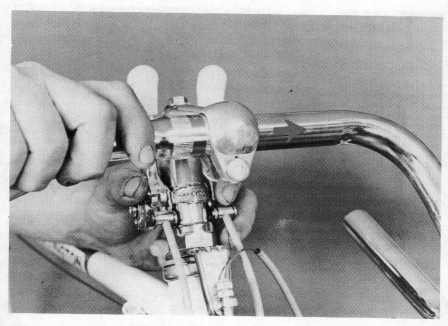

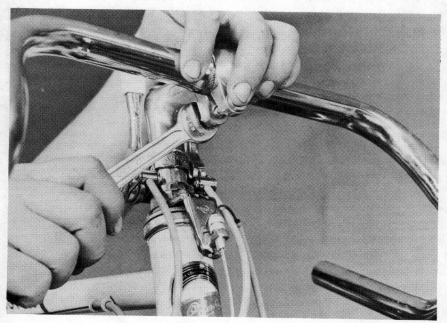

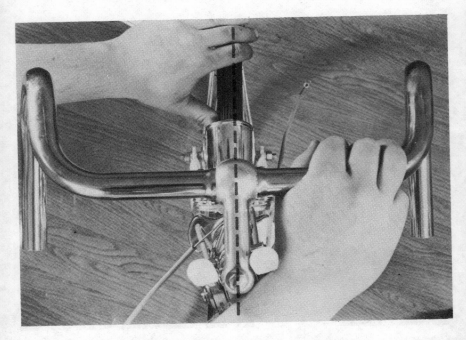

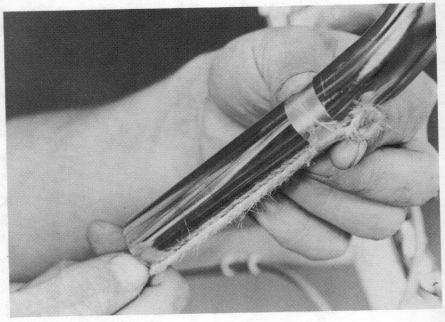

Comfortable riding depends on suitable alignment of the handlebars drop. Here is a method that assures exactly the right angle. Tape a string where the hands will grip. Stretch the string straight. Rotate the handlebar in the clamp until the string, in line with the grip, bisects the rear hub. Some experts can make this alignment by eye, but a string removes doubt. One caution: do not fudge. The string must align with the grips exactly. Tighten the clamp so the handlebars cannot move. Recheck alignment of the crossbar, and tighten the stem bolt so the stem cannot turn without the fork.

Touring handlebars exhibit a different configuration. The grips, instead of pointing downward, rest flat. They take rubber handlebar grips. Otherwise, flat handlebars install about the same as the *maes-bend* variety.

Move the stem shifters to a point just above the head nut. Let the handles extend not more than an inch above the stem bolt. Center them on the stem, and tighten the clamp. They operate the derailleurs, and that section (covered in section 5) deals with adjusting the shifters as well as the derailleurs. Some shifters hang on the frame, near the top of the front tube. Since they are not involved with the handlebar stem, they are usually mounted at the factory.

At this point, if you are assembling a new bike, you mount the brake levers, before you tape the handlebars. Safety levers, if the bike has them, go on after the taping. In a maintenance overhaul, however, you work with brake levers and safety levers right along with the brakes. You will find them covered in Section 2 of book 2.

Tape on the handlebars provides the rider a firm gripping surface. The tape is special plastic, and comes in a roll with just enough tape for one bicycle.

Completely unroll the tape and pass one end around the seat tube of the bicycle and divide the tape into two equal strips. That way, you will have the same amount for both sides.

Begin next to the center. Take one full wrap in the direction of the center clamp which is the anchor wrap. Then begin wrapping toward the handlebar curve. Wrap that first couple of turns with considerable overlap, so that it will hold the anchor wrap securely. The tape has a bit of stretch built in; wrap it firmly and tightly.

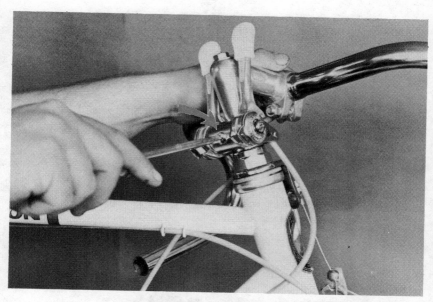

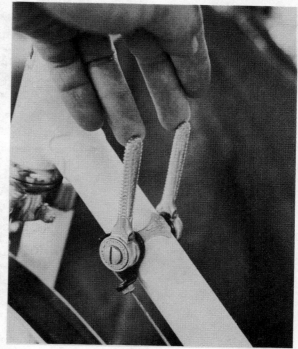

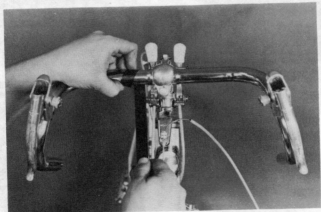

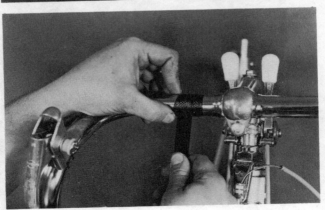

Overlap the tape between ⅛ and ¼ inch as you continue wrapping the straight section. Most people run into trouble on the bend, where the handlebar curves forward toward the brake lever. The secret, which may seem obvious to some, lies in overlapping the tape more on the inside of the curve than on the outside. Maintain a ⅛-inch overlap on the outer radius of the curve, but let the overlap broaden enough on the inside radius to keep the angle of wrapping about the same right on around the curve.

Then comes the brake lever. When the normal wrap of the tape brings it up against the brake lever clamp, lengthen the turn underneath the clamp. Stretch the tape a bit extra tight here. That brings you right out on the other side, and you can continue wrapping toward the end.

The handlebar end offers another tough spot for the un-initiated. It is not especially easy for the experienced. The main trick is coming out with the right amount of tape at the end—neither too much nor too little. Cut off all but 4 inches of any excess.

The last few turns should be tight and overlapped a little extra, maybe ¼ inch or so. At the very end, let the tape over-lap the end bar about ⅜ inch. Take a couple of turns with that overlap, and then tuck the free end into the open end of the handlebar tube.

Push that free end as far into the tube as your finger can reach. That length of tape anchors the whole wrapping job. Then, carefully, crimp the overlap into the tube end. If you do it smoothly, the tape nearly covers the tubing edges.

All that is left is to plug the handlebar end. A rubber or plastic plug comes with the tape. Insert it in the end, making sure that it binds the tape evenly around the hole. Push the plug as far in as you can by hand.

Then when you're sure the tape is held evenly, take a rub-ber mallet and "set" the plug. (Some end plugs have a bolt expanding; you set them with a screwdriver.) This makes a nice smooth fit, with tape snug all the way from center clamp to handlebar tip. Repeat with the other half of the handlebar.

In the sequence of assembling a bicycle, this seems a good time to mount the kickstand. You have finished working

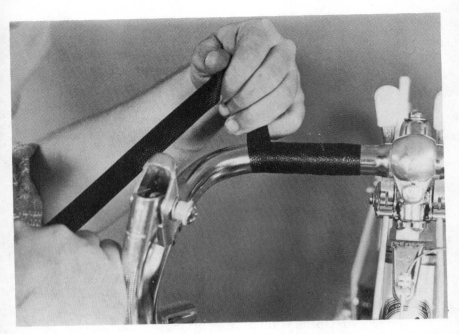

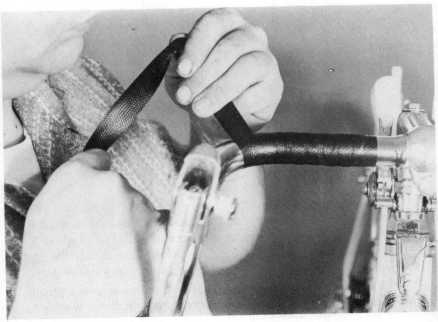

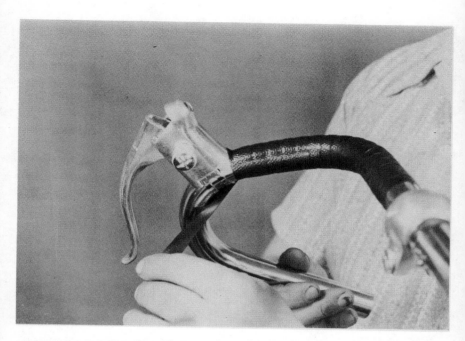

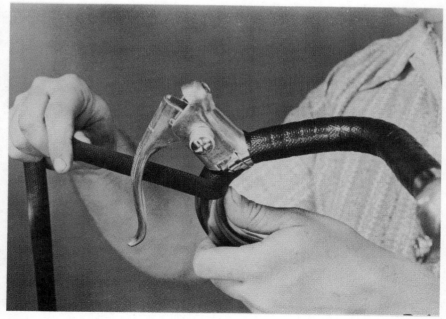

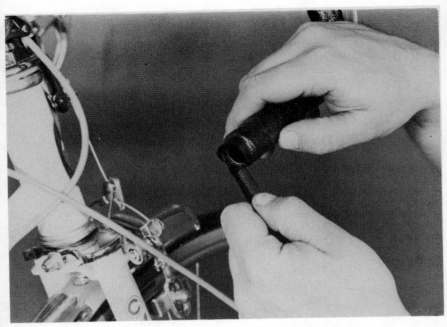

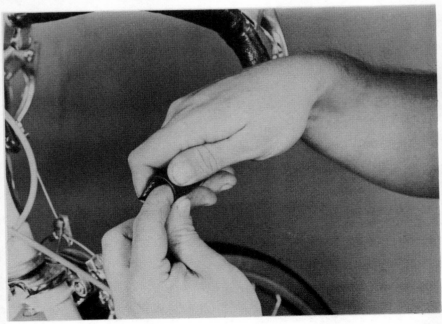

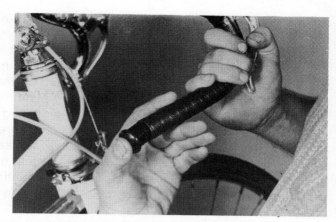

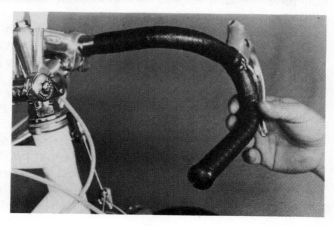

around the crank, and the kickstand will not get in the way of other work you have yet to do.

There is not much to it. Remove the nut from the mounting bolt and then remove the mounting plate; it has curves to fit the front of the chain stays. Fit the kickstand on the bottom of the gap in the stays. Slide the mounting plate down over the bolt, then a lockwasher, and then the mounting nut.

Tighten the nut, but not overly tight. Too much pressure on the mounting plate mashes the chain stays, weakening the frame. Worse, the bent stays would throw the rear end out of line and eventually ruin the rear hub. The mounting needs very little pressure to hold up the bike when it's on the kickstand.

Once a year, in your maintenance overhaul, you should remove the seat post. You should also remove it when you are assembling a new bicycle. Taking it out may not be entirely easy.

Begin by loosening the clamp at the top of the seat tube. Then, if the post happens to be stuck—and it usually is—grip it tightly with *Channellock®* pliers and tap upward with a hammer. If the post was installed right, a few firm taps should suffice. Lift the post out completely.

Look closely at the clamp at the top of the seat tube. Often the edge projects above the top of the tube—that's bad. Work the clamp down until the seat extends through the clamp only slightly . . . say 1/16 inch. The clamp and the seat tube may have irregular edges; the clamp must be below the top of the tube as shown in the illustration.

One step you absolutely must remember with the seat post. **OIL IT WELL** before you reinsert it in the seat tube. The post material rusts and so does the material in the tube. Between the two of them, you need a coating of oil, otherwise they rust together. When this happens you cannot adjust seat height, or remove the post if it gets bent in a spill. So rub the seat post generously with oil.

You will also find a depth mark on most seat posts. Make sure the post goes into the tube at least that far. The same rule-of-thumb applies as for the handlebar stem: as much in the tube as out. Once the saddle is on, you can refine the height adjustment. (If the seat post has to be raised too high,

70

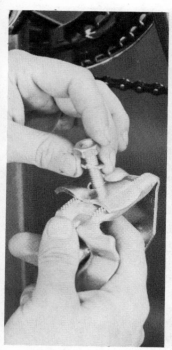

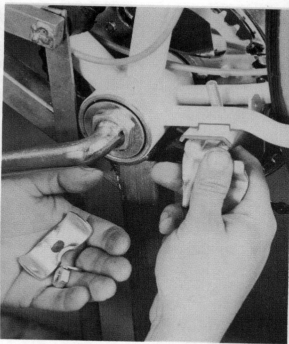

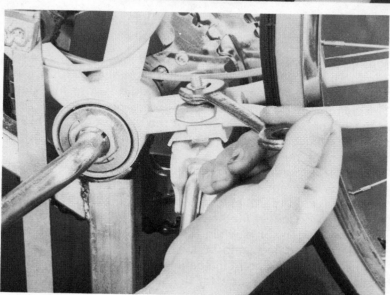

your bike frame is too small for you; too low, the frame is too large.) Snug down the clamp, but not too tight.

Examine the bottom side of the saddle before installing. The clamp may be turned backward; they often are. The hole in the clamp should be forward of the clamp bolt, not to the rear of it. Loosen the bolt and turn the clamp forward. Set the saddle on the post and fasten the clamp loosely.

Comfort in normal riding dictates that the saddle be level. Ignore the bow and adjust the saddle tilt so a yardstick laid across it extends parallel to the top tube of the bicycle frame. You can ("fine tune") tilt the saddle later, if you need to, after you have ridden for a while. Level usually works out best. Tighten the saddle clamp bolt.

Now you reach a point in seat adjustment that has two factors to consider. One, how far the saddle should be from the

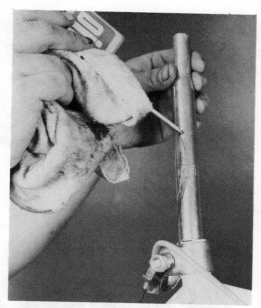

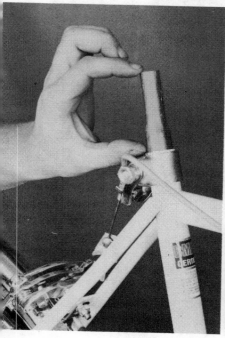

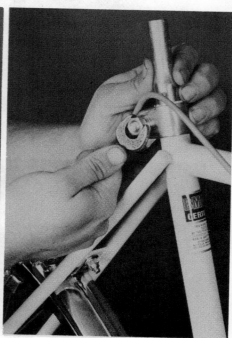

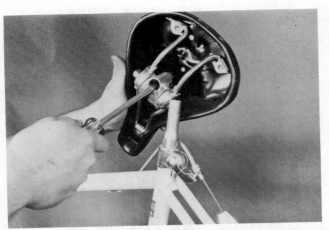

pedals. Two, the relationship between saddle and
handlebars. The first usually gets primary attention.

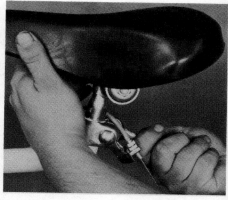

Loosen the seat post
clamp at the top of the seat
tube. Place the saddle at a
height (by sliding the post
up or down) that sets your
heel solidly on a pedal, with
the pedal at its lowest posi-
tion. Tighten the seat post
clamp.

Next set the relationship between the saddle and the handlebars. A yardstick between the two can establish their rela-
tive positions. Let the yardstick lay across the saddle, parallel
to the top tube. Note where it falls between the stem shifters.
Raise or lower the stem to set the handlebars (and recheck
stem alignment as described earlier (Section 3). Tighten the
stem bolt.

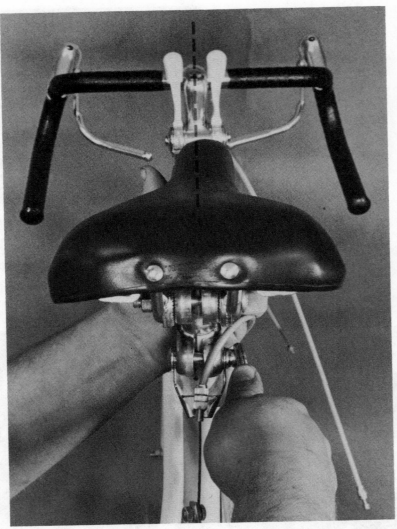

Finally, set the angle of the saddle. Loosen the saddle clamp slightly and aim the saddle directly between the shifters. Tighten the saddle clamp and retighten the seat post clamp.

Touring bicycles generally have mattress saddles. They are shaped differently than racing saddles, and have more padding. Alignment follows the same principles.

Another handy way to check the relationship between saddle and handlebar involves a string. Loop the string over the stem neck and around the handlebar clamp. Stretch it taut to the rear of the saddle. The string should run parallel to the top tube of the frame, and saddle tilt should be level with the string.

Adjustment to achieve proper saddle/handlebar alignment are the same as just described for racing saddles. The saddle clamp lets you set angle and tilt; the seat post determines height. Once you adjust seat height to put the pedals in reach of your feet, you can refine handlebar height.

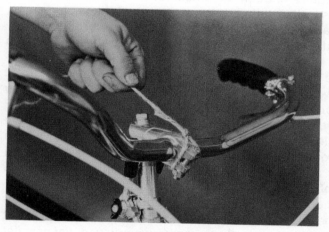

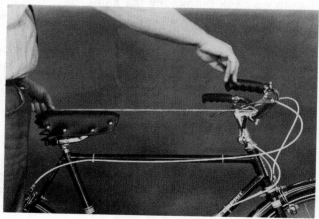

SECTION 4

Tires

Tires require enough air pressure, an occasional inspection, and sensible riding. If the rest of the bike is shipshape, the tires last out their normal life with little other attention.

About the worst tire defect that is likely to sneak up on you is an angled valve stem, caused by tire and tube creeping on the rim. If that happens, it is important that you correct it right away. The tube pinches and wears out quickly if you do not correct it as soon as possible.

The wheel does not necessarily have to be removed from the bicycle to align a valve stem—but we will cover where removal for all practical purposes since it must be done when replacing a tire. If you do a lot of road riding, you'll want a new set of tires at least once a year.

Take the front wheel out of the fork. Pay particular attention to the order in which the hub hardware comes off. It has to go back on exactly the same way: keyed washer, flat washer, lockwasher, and nut. (For rear wheel demounting, see Section 2).

For removing the tire, you will need three bicycle tire irons. Never use a screwdriver as a replacement; you will damage the tube either removing it or putting it back in. You can also damage the tire bead.

Deflate the inner tube. Insert the rounded end of the first tire iron down into the rim and under the bead of the tire. Pry downward, which brings the tire bead up and outside the rim. At the bent end of the tire iron you will see a slot. Hook that around a spoke to hold the iron in place. About 4 inches away, insert another tire iron the same way. Pry the bead out with it, and again hook the bent end around a spoke.

Finally, slip the third tire iron under the bead end and scoot it all the way around the wheel. The tire bead should pop out fairly easily with this procedure.

With all of the tire bead outside the rim, you can extract the inner tube. Start opposite the valve stem, and pull the tube out and downward. When you have the tube about halfway out, you can also peel the whole tire from the rim, starting again opposite the valve stem. Having stripped both tire and tube off the wheel, slip the valve stem free of its hole.

Incidentally, while the tire is off, there is no better time to haul the wheels to your favorite bicycle shop and have them "tuned up." The technician has the tools, equipment, and know-how to test and correct wheel roundness and alignment. This should always be done for both wheels when you put on new tires, or at the start of each riding season.

Always install a rim strip between the inner tube and the rim of the wheel. This prevents excessive wear on the tube.

The rim strip is rubber. Locate the valve stem hole and place it right over the hole in the rim. Keeping the holes aligned, stretch the strip around the wheel. Work the strip so its tension is the same all the way around; otherwise it eventually puts strain on the inner tube. Also make sure the strip lies flat, with no curls along the edges.

One mysterious cause of tube punctures traces to a spoke projecting through its nipple. Such a spoke is too long to start with. If threaded into the nipple and adjusted with the tire on the rim, you cannot see the end working its way up into the rim strip and inner tube.

The cure is simple and straightforward. Just grip the offending spoke end down close to the rim with pliers, bend it back and forth a few times, and break it off. Make sure it is flush. Then restore the rim strip over it.

Examine the new (or patched) tube for installation by inflating it slightly, just enough to round it out. Start at the valve stem and press the tube into the tire. Smooth it into the tire all the way around, and make sure there are no kinks.

When you are satisfied of the fit, insert the valve stem into its hole in the wheel. Press it down firmly. Pull from the underside, wiggling the stem and working it down for a snug fit in the hole.

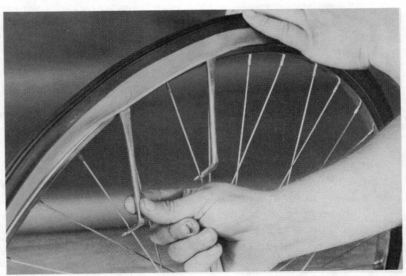

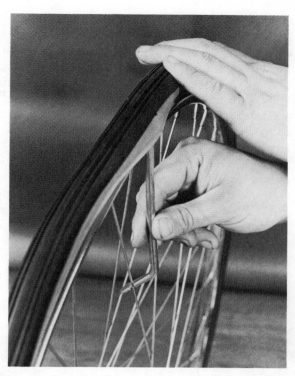

Probably the handiest way to tuck the first bead into the rim, if your arms are long enough, is to pick up the whole wheel and tire. Hold the valve side against you, and start sliding the bead in. The first bead goes quickly and easily.

After one bead is on the rim all the way around, run your finger around inside to make sure the inner tube has distributed itself evenly. It should be round and without kinks anywhere. Recheck the valve stem to be sure it is snug and straight.

Then, beginning at the valve stem, start pressing the other bead into place. Work your way further and further from the stem in both directions, until you reach the point where just pushing with your thumbs will not snap the bead into the rim.

Use tire irons to work the rest of the bead into place. You can hold the tire with one iron and pry with the other. Around the sidewall of most tires, maybe ⅛ inch from the wheel rim, you will see a ridge either molded or painted onto the tire. That is to guide you in seating the beads in the rim. This line should be equidistant from the rim all the way around the

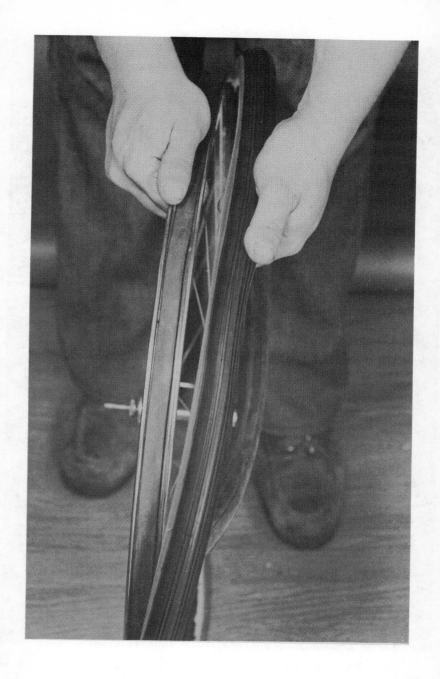

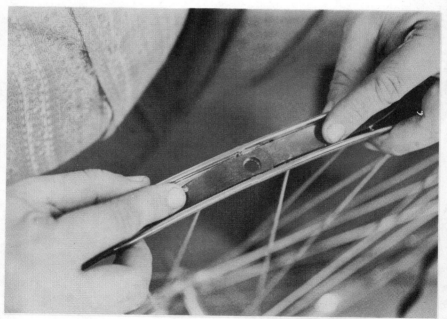

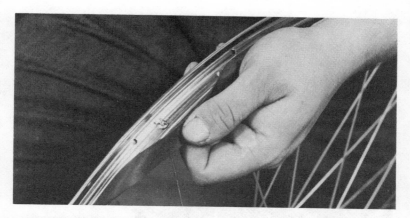

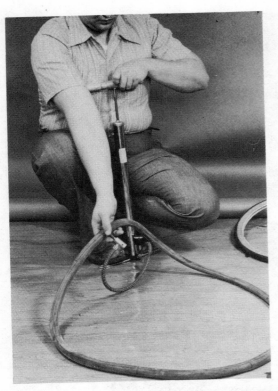

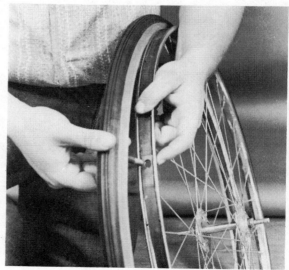

tire. That assures proper centering and balance for the tire.

Inflate the tire in steps. Pump it up a little and recheck the tire centering (preceding page). Then bounce it a couple of times on the floor to help the tube expand evenly without kinks. Add some more air and recheck centering. Inflate the tire to whatever pressure you find stamped on its sidewall. Pressures differ widely for various tires, so you can never be sure what pressure might be required. It can range from 60 lb. to more than 100. As a safe rule, you can pressure any tires on a ten-speed bicycle to 60 lbs.

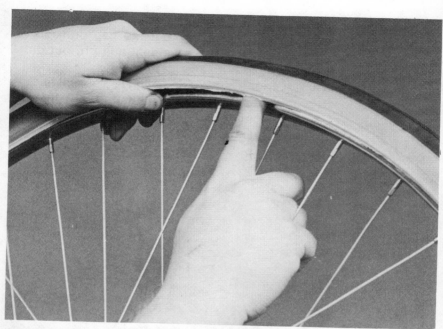

As one last step, screw the valve cap on. Valves in bicycle tires do not develop much problem, but the cap prevents leakage from that source. It also keeps dust and grit out of the valve. Never ride without a valve cap.

Reinstall the wheel on the bicycle and align it. You will find help with those procedures in Section 2. You are ready then to mount and ride in comfort and safety. Go through the maintenance and adjustment suggestions in this book once a year, and you can ride confident that your machine delivers its best performance.

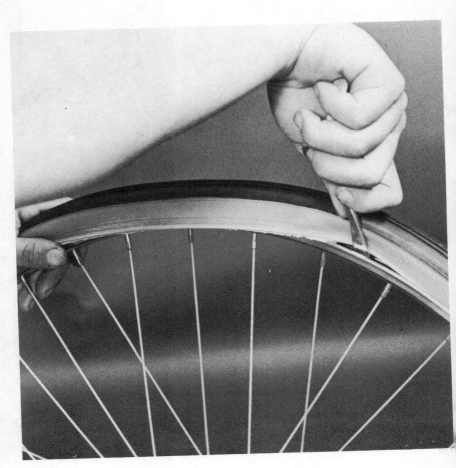

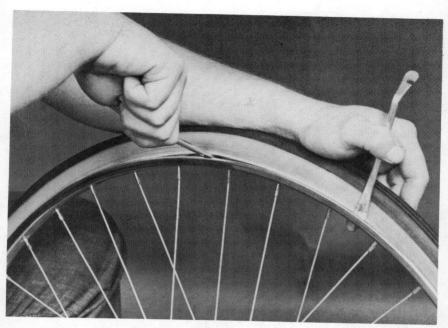

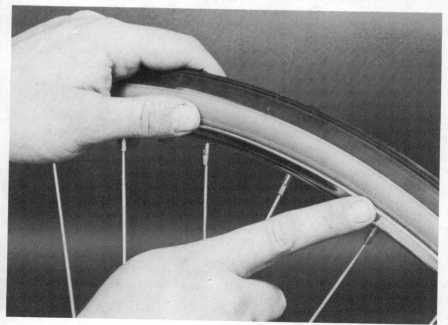

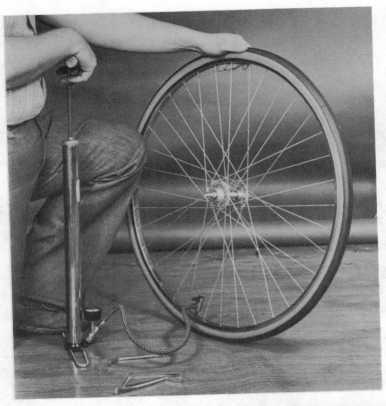

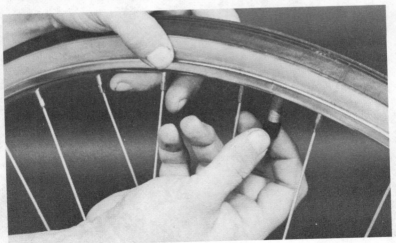